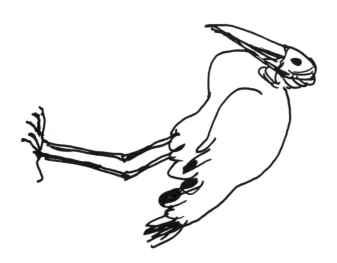

D1411041

A Wood Stork Named Warren

(A Fable of Nature and God)

NANCY S. BRESLIN

art / BOB HODGELL

Prokaryote Press
P.O. Box 66362
St. Petersburg Beach, FL 33736-6362

ISBN 0-9630911-0-7

Library of Congress Catalog Card Number 91-62203

Printed in the United States of America on recycled paper with soybean ink.

First Edition

Dedication

For "ORANGE BAND," Earth's last Dusky Seaside Sparrow, who died in a cage at Disney World June 16, 1987, after seven years in captivity. He was tiny and fragile and sang a special song. We loved spaceships more.

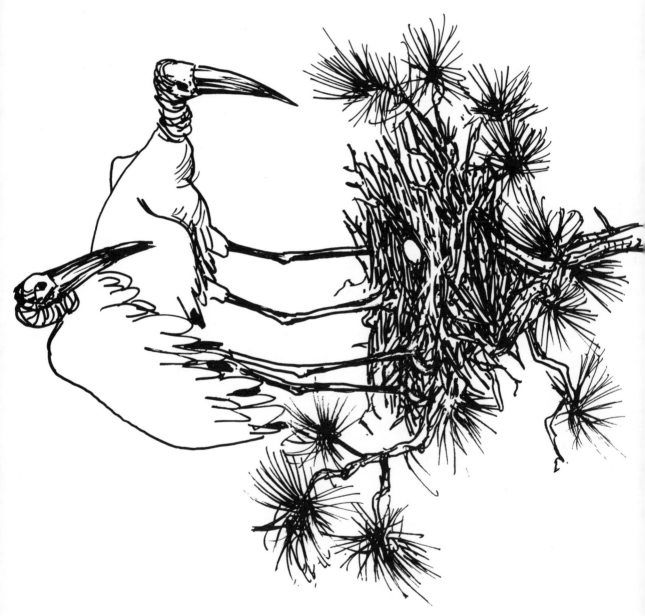

1.

The creatures of the wetland celebrated being in extraordinary ways. Glossy lilypads floated on dark pools where mosquitofish and alligators swam. Owls flew silently into nights without moonlight. Lush air plants thrived. Brilliant dragonflies darted through misty stillness. Tiny frogs made great sounds. Spiders spun elaborate webs. Mosses and snails decorated gnarled branches. Insects skated over water. . . . And, in a large nest atop the tallest tree, a wood stork named Warren broke apart his eggshell.

2.

Warren's early days were peaceful. His parents cared for him well. They fed him fish, frogs, and crayfish they caught in the nearby pools. To protect his delicate body from the sun and rain they stood above him and stretched out their great wings. And on the hottest days, they even carried up water to his nest in their throats and trickled it over him.

Soft gray down covered Warren at first, but as time passed, stronger feathers appeared - - brilliant white on his body, a wide band of iridescent black and green on his wings and tail, and brown on his neck and head. He had gray eyes, a sturdy yellowish beak which curved downward, and long gray legs with pink feet. Warren was a marvelous being. And as are all creatures, he was unlike any other who ever had been or would be on earth.

Warren quickly grew old enough to fly. Spreading and flapping his strong broad wings and stretching out his body as straight as an arrow came easy to him. Soon he was gliding long distances through the sky, looking down on the beautiful world below as the sun warmed his wings. Afterwards he rested, safe in the branches of the wetland trees.

Warren also began catching his own fish. He would wade in the shallow water and shuffle his pink feet. Then by opening his beak and moving it from side to side, he captured creatures startled out of the waterweeds. Often he fished alone. But he preferred fishing with the other wetland birds and those coming there at times from places far away.

Warren had a wonderful life, and he enjoyed it as only he could. The wetland gave him food and shelter and the freedom and privacy to be all a wood stork can be.

3.

For billions of years, God has loved all who are or ever have been on earth. Because He is so loving, He does not determine what they become. Instead they have freedom. They are free to act on their own to become different from the creatures He wants them to be. And also they are free to seek God's help to become those creatures He wants them to be. By guiding the creatures who seek His help, God creates on earth and makes life on it more perfect.

Many creatures do not let God guide them and so are different from

11

the creatures He wants them to be. They cause whatever is disorderly and imperfect on the earth and do not make life on it better. But there are many others who do seek God's guidance. With His help, they become creatures who improve their own lives and the lives of others. They cause whatever is orderly and perfect on the earth and make life on it better. Many of these creatures live in the wetland. God has linked their lives together. He has created each to give care to others. And each is cared for by others He has created to give it care.

God has created wood storks and they care for others in so many ways. They provide food and homes for much smaller creatures. They make some of the air the plants breathe, and they breathe some of the air the plants make. They safeguard others' food and space. They enrich the soil. They are companions for countless creatures. They nest with each other and bring the wetland new generations. They feed, protect, and teach their chicks. They bring beauty, uniqueness, and variety. . . . Wood storks make life on earth better.

4.

The years passed, bringing the wetland many seasons of rain and dryness. In this time, Warren flew and fished and grew into one of its largest birds. He now stood over three feet tall and could spread his wings almost twice that far. Gray skin had replaced the feathers on his neck and head and his beak had darkened. Soon, like the millions of wood storks who had lived in the wetland before him, he would be old enough to find a mate and raise a family. Perhaps they too would nest atop the wetland's tallest tree.

Warren was aware of nothing which could keep him from raising a family in the wetland. His world had been the same world of those millions of wood storks before him. For as long as it had existed, the wetland had been a place untouched by the creatures who bring sudden change.

5.

The following dry season, near the time Warren would find his mate and begin building their nest, humans entered the wetland. The wetland creatures had never seen beings like them. Humans were earth's most powerful creatures for they knew how to disturb or destroy all life on it.

The humans brought with them some of the mighty tools they had learned to build and use -- bulldozers, dredges, earthmovers, steamrollers, trucks, and chainsaws. These machines made noises which drowned out the grunt of the alligator, the woodpecker's call, and the rustle of leaves in the wind. . . . But the humans had not come into the wetland to make noises.

15

The humans used their machines to clear away the wetland plants. The tallest tree, who had survived hundreds of years of storms, droughts, and diseases, stood defenseless before them. The nest in which Warren had hatched, and the countless others the great tree had protected for so long, fell with it to the ground. . . . All plants and most creatures in them were killed.

The humans used their machines to drain and fill with dirt the places in the wetland which collected rain. One by one Warren's fishing holes disappeared. . . . Most creatures in and near the water were killed.

The humans used their machines to pave over the dirt and build with glass, asphalt, concrete, steel, and plastic. They created roads, businesses, farms, and houses to replace even the open areas where the larger wetland animals had roamed and over which Warren had flown with grace and freedom. . . . Most creatures above and under the ground were killed.

ONCE LIVING ON EARTH AND FILLING IT WITH WONDROUS CELEBRATION, THE WETLAND AND MOST OF ITS CREATURES WERE NOW GONE FOREVER. NOT EVEN EARTH'S MOST POWERFUL BEINGS COULD BRING BACK THOSE THEY HAD DESTROYED.

6.

WHY HAD THE WETLAND AND ITS CREATURES BEEN DESTROYED? GOD LOVED THEM. HE HELPED THEM BECOME THE CREATURES HE WANTED THEM TO BE. . . . BUT GOD LOVES ALL CREATURES, EVEN HUMANS. HE HELPS HUMANS TOO BECOME THE CREATURES HE WANTS THEM TO BE. . . . HAD GOD HELPED THESE HUMANS BECOME CREATURES WHO DESTROY OTHERS AS THEY HAD? . . . OR WERE THEY ACTING WITHOUT GOD'S HELP AND DIFFERENTLY FROM HOW HE WANTS THEM TO BE?

17

7.

Warren was alive. In the weeks following the humans' arrival in the wetland, he had found places to hide in the surrounding territory and had watched them destroy the only home he had ever known. His security, his privacy, and his usual sources of food and shelter were gone. He was very frightened and confused and weak from lack of food and rest. Most of the wetland creatures who also had escaped already had perished. They had known the dangers in their wetland home and where to find food and shelter there. But in the unfamiliar human territory to which they had fled, they had not found food and shelter easily nor been able to recognize or avoid its dangers. Soon, unless Warren found another wetland or adapted better to places humans create, he too would die.

Warren was about to fly far away when something incredible happened. An astounding change came over him, filling him with knowledge and abilities no wood stork ever before had possessed. It made him more aware of who he was and what existed around him. It gave him greater understanding not only that he was separate from his surroundings but also that he was part of the world in which he lived. And it made him better able to think and remember as the human creatures could. But perhaps strangest of all, it gave him the ability to comprehend their language and to ask a question in that language no nonhuman creature ever had spoken. Yet not until a strong wind placed him before several of the humans now inhabiting his wetland, did he realize this question was meant for them.

Warren's unexpected appearance surprised the humans and a large crowd formed around him. The shy wood stork was terrified. He knew he was now different from all other wood storks, but he did not know how or why he had been changed or what lay ahead. He also knew he could have flown away, but what had happened had convinced him that asking his question was more important than his safety, so he chose to stay. And even though his body shook uncontrollably and his heart pounded, from somewhere came the courage he needed to do what he had decided he must. In a small and halting voice, he uttered six human words - - "WHY DID YOU DESTROY MY HOME?"

9.

(Warren amazed all humans who ever saw and heard him. Many ridiculed him. Others reacted with fear. Yet some answered his question.)

Several in the crowd told Warren that they were developers and that the wetland belonged to them and some farmers because they had paid money for it. They said it had been worth nothing to them as it was, but they had made it valuable by changing it into land without plants, animals, and water. Then on the part they owned, they had been able to put up many buildings. And by selling and renting the buildings, they not only made a good living for themselves and their families but also created more jobs for humans, more houses in which humans could live, more businesses where humans could shop, and more places where humans could be entertained. They said they had even made enough money developing their part of the wetland to buy more wetlands to develop. Then they suggested that Warren hear also from the farmers. Warren flew away. . . . BUT THE DEVELOPERS NEVER FORGOT HIM. HIS QUESTION HAD TROUBLED THEIR HEARTS.

10.

Warren found the farmers nearby and asked them his question − −
"WHY DID YOU DESTROY MY HOME?"

The farmers told Warren that the number of humans on earth was increasing very rapidly and that the easiest way to supply the crops and meat they demanded was to transform more of the earth into places where human food could be grown. This meant changing forests and wetlands like his into farms or into areas where waste from farms could run off or be dumped. They said that by growing and selling crops and livestock on the part of his wetland they had changed into farms they also were able to make a good living for themselves and their families. They told Warren that they and the developers had gotten permission from politicians to develop and farm his wetland and directed him to the city where the politicians worked. Warren flew away. . . . BUT THE FARMERS NEVER FORGOT HIM. HIS QUESTION HAD TROUBLED THEIR HEARTS.

11.

Not even the wetland's destruction had frightened Warren as much as the city to which he had flown to find the politicians. He was surrounded by crowds of humans, towering buildings, and streets where traffic roared by. There was noise everywhere and few trees in whose branches he could rest or hide. But finally he found the politicians, and asked them his question - - "WHY DID YOU DESTROY MY HOME?"

A couple of the politicians laughed and told Warren that since he was only a bird they would be honest with him. They said they needed money and votes to get and keep their jobs. So in exchange for the money and votes of the developers and farmers, they had given them what they had asked for - - permission to develop and farm his wetland. Others told Warren that they had permitted the development and farming of his wetland because they felt it was best for the citizens they represented. It would bring them more jobs, more businesses, more houses, and more tax money to pay for more services. They said they had done only what those citizens wanted them to do. Most citizens supported the development and farming of his wetland, either because they believed it would bring them more of what was important to them, or because they did not care what happened to it. The politicians told Warren how to find a family of citizens to hear their views for himself. Warren flew away. . . . BUT THE POLITICIANS NEVER FORGOT HIM. HIS QUESTION HAD TROUBLED THEIR HEARTS.

12.

Warren found the family of citizens in a house on the city's outskirts and asked them his question -- "WHY DID YOU DESTROY MY HOME?"

The father told Warren that what happened to his wetland had been for politicians to decide and so was not his concern. He did feel, however, that if humans were going to destroy wetlands, a number of the creatures living there should be captured in case humans ever wanted them for research or entertainment. The mother told Warren that she believed that the earth and all creatures on it had been made by God. She said that she wanted to live on the earth as He intended. She believed God intended humans to have comfortable lives and to care for other humans and felt this meant having whatever more they could get by developing and farming Warren's wetland. The son said their religious leaders told them about God but had said nothing to cause them to question the destruction of his wetland. He said he believed that God had put so many wetlands on the earth humans could never destroy them all. And the daughter said that even if humans destroyed all wetlands, God would create more. All of them told Warren they were sorry they needed to take his home and suggested he visit their religious leaders. Warren flew away. . . . BUT THE FAMILY NEVER FORGOT HIM. HIS QUESTION HAD TROUBLED THEIR HEARTS.

13.

Warren found the family's religious leaders not far away and asked them his question -- "WHY DID YOU DESTROY MY HOME?"

One of the leaders told Warren that he believed humans were the only creatures important to God and that He did not care how they treated everything else on earth. He said that humans were able to love, but that loving did not include caring for the earth or for nonhuman creatures. Yet another told Warren she believed that God loves wetlands and all creatures, and that humans can love them as He does. She said she had never tried to help humans understand this because it conflicted with how most chose to live and with what her organization wanted her to do. One said he had told the humans that caring for the earth and its creatures was their duty to God. And another confessed that he had not studied and listened enough to learn how to tell humans what God is really like so that they would love Him enough to learn to love all others. The religious leaders hurried away after they spoke. . . . BUT THEY NEVER FORGOT WARREN. HIS QUESTION HAD TROUBLED THEIR HEARTS.

14.

Warren walked away. He was exhausted from his journeys and did not have enough strength to fly. His wings felt very heavy, as if they were made of the humans' concrete. Only a short time ago he had been a shy wetland creature who had never seen humans. But now, for a reason still unknown to him, he had been changed, traveled miles in human territory, and listened to them explain why they had destroyed his home. He wished he had never been able to ask the humans his question or understand their answers. They had shown him no hatred and most had been kind. He had liked many of them. But he had found out something he could not bear - - that they could love but had not loved the wetland and its creatures. They had not respected them or shown consideration for them in any way.

Warren did not know what to do or where to go. He began walking in the direction of his beautiful wetland home. But he suddenly stopped when he remembered that the place to which he desperately longed to return no longer existed. And springing directly from his anguish and pain, a new question formed in his mind - - "WHY AREN'T WOOD STORKS AND WETLANDS WORTH LOVING?"

Warren believed this question would never be answered. He wanted to hear nothing more from the humans. And at the moment God seemed very far away. Deep despair and loneliness, dark feelings no wood stork had ever before experienced, overwhelmed him, and his heart felt as if it were breaking. In weariness and sorrow, he lowered his head and great tears streamed down his beak.

33

15.

It was then that God let Warren know He was there with him. In His quiet and gentle way, God told Warren that He had always loved him and that He would never stop loving him. He said He loved Warren so much that at every moment of Warren's life He knew everything that was happening to him. Because He loved the wetland and its creatures so much, He had rejoiced with them as they celebrated being. But now, because they had been destroyed and made to suffer by the humans, He was filled with great sadness and loss.

God explained to Warren that He had changed him. He had made him the only wood stork ever to have human abilities and feelings. He had changed Warren because He wanted to try a new way of reaching out to some humans who needed help. They did not understand that they could be creatures who love the earth and all others. Nor did they understand that the earth and all creatures really needed their love. He wanted Warren to reach out to them because Warren lived in a wetland they had not loved and because he was a wood stork, a creature disappearing from the earth because humans have not loved it. God said that He had made Warren able to speak the question these humans needed to hear and that Warren had made Him very happy when he had not flown away but had done so well the difficult job of asking it.

Then God explained to Warren that, just as He loved him, He also loved the humans very much. He wanted them to know Him and to love and trust Him and let Him help them to love others. But even He could not make them love and trust Him because these things come from making choices. Love comes from choosing between loving and not loving, and trust comes from choosing between trusting and not trusting. Humans had the freedom they needed to make these choices. Only they could decide whether they would love Him and all creatures as He could teach them, or whether they would live selfish lives.

God said that because humans could know Him and let Him love and teach them, if they did not take the love and guidance He wanted to give them, they would not be all they could be. They would be like wood storks who never flew! He was always telling them this. Many had listened and come to understand how much they needed His love and guidance and that they could love every creature on earth. Some had not learned as much and believed they could love only humans. Still others had learned little and felt that happiness came from living selfishly. They pushed God away and believed they knew better than He what would make them happy. God told Warren that it broke His heart whenever humans decided to live selfishly or to limit the love they gave. They would not find the happiness they seek and they would keep others from having the love they need. Many of these humans were causing great harm to the earth and all creatures on it.

They were pumping chemicals, garbage, and waste into the water He has created, polluting it so that creatures cannot drink or live in it without harm. They were pouring chemicals and emissions into the air He has created, poisoning it so that creatures cannot breathe or fly in it without harm. They were neglecting and dumping waste into the soil He has created, wearing it out, contaminating it, and causing it to be blown or washed away to places where it did damage or could not be useful. And by not caring for the air, water, and soil, they were greatly harming all the creatures He has created. But even worse, many times they were harming them intentionally or were failing to act when they needed help. They even had caused countless numbers to disappear from the earth and now were threatening many others, like the unique and wonderful wood stork and the complex and beautiful wetland.

16.

The moment God had begun speaking, the great love in His voice had dried Warren's tears. In just this brief time, He had given Warren some awareness of the way in which humans could know Him. Warren now understood that humans had the freedom to choose to love and that some did not give love as they could but limited their love or acted selfishly. But he no longer felt alone. He knew for sure that God loved him, was always with him, and wanted wood storks to enjoy their lives on earth and improve life for others. Warren knew that the wood stork's future was uncertain

and that it would be determined by the choices humans make. But he no longer despaired. He realized now that God's love for the earth and its creatures was so great that He would always be present and reaching out to them. He would always be trying to tell the humans how deeply He loves them and how they can find happiness by learning to become creatures who love others, including wood storks and wetlands, as much as they can. And Warren now knew that many humans had listened to God and were trying to live in this way.

The work for which God had changed Warren was finished. Because he understood now that God had chosen him to reach out to humans in an extraordinary way, joy had replaced his sorrow. Yet Warren found being in their world very difficult and looked forward to God's returning him to the wood stork world in which he belonged. He had only one regret - - that he had not gotten to visit some of the humans who knew God and were giving their love to the earth and all creatures.

God understood what was in Warren's heart. He too wanted him to meet humans who loved wood storks and wetlands.

17.

Suddenly two creatures of different colors, shapes, and sizes approached. When Warren heard them speaking the same human language he knew, he realized that God had sent them and smiled a wood stork smile.

The animal with soft tawny fur, a long tail, and beautiful eyes spoke first.

"Humans call me a panther. Not long ago my family spread over a large area of the earth, searching at night for our food. But then humans came to hunt us and take away the land on which we lived, and we fled

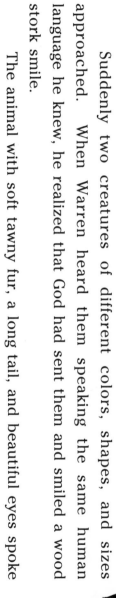

into the wilderness. Now they have come into the wilderness to hunt us and take away that land. Only a few of us are still alive. We have nowhere left to go and probably will not live on earth much longer."

The second creature then spoke. His skin was smooth and bluish gray and his head was very large. From the roof of his mouth hung fringe-like sheets of horn.

"Humans call me a whale. My family travels long distances in the oceans eating tiny creatures we strain through the sheets in our mouths. But now there are few whales like us in the sea. For thousands of years humans have hunted us for meat and oil, and after they began using fast ships and harpoons and polluting the waters, they killed almost all of us."

Yet the panther and the whale told Warren there were humans who loved them, and they led him to a development. Its developer greeted them with kindness, and they listened quietly as he spoke of the way he lived on the earth.

"God wants us earthly creatures to live here without causing harm. Many are taught to do this by their parents and relatives. Humans too are

taught this way, and by other humans and nonhumans as well. We also learn by seeing the harm we do whenever our acts interfere with the order and balance of the world God is creating. I will give you a good example.

"God has created trees to give the earth many things. Trees breathe some of the air the animals make and make some of the air the animals breathe. They collect the sun's heat in cool times and in warm times they release water to cool the air. They hold dirt around their roots to keep wind and water from carrying it away. They give creatures food, shelter, and shade. They absorb pollution. They bring beauty, color, and quiet. And even after they die, they enrich the soil. But we humans have seen when we cut down a great many trees, there are not enough left to do everything they were created to do. So we humans learn that by cutting down that many trees, we are causing harm. We are keeping the trees from being the creatures God made them to be, and we are keeping ourselves and others from having all that God created trees to give.

"Humans also learn how to live on the earth without causing harm when we get to know God well enough to discover that all of the creatures who improve life here have been created out of His goodness and love. They

should be cherished and protected. When we extinguish forever even one, all of us left have lost a being who would have enriched our lives.

"Humans have freedom to make many many decisions about the way we live and care for the earth. God wants us to make decisions which improve life, not only for humans but for the nonhuman creatures sharing the earth with us. If humans don't make decisions which improve life for all creatures, we take away from those others the care we can give them. And we take away from ourselves the joy that comes from caring for them, as well as the countless benefits to be received from their being cared for by us.

"Each time I consider developing part of the earth, I first decide the best I can that it would not be doing harm by interfering with the order and balance God is creating here. When I do develop, I have been able to leave most of the natural area unchanged. This way I disturb the land's plants and animals as little as possible and provide the humans who come there to live or work with the peace, beauty, and sense of community those creatures bring. I also make sure I put equipment on the land to store and dispose of anything harmful to it. And I clean up anything harmful which may have been left there before I came. I could make much more money by getting rid

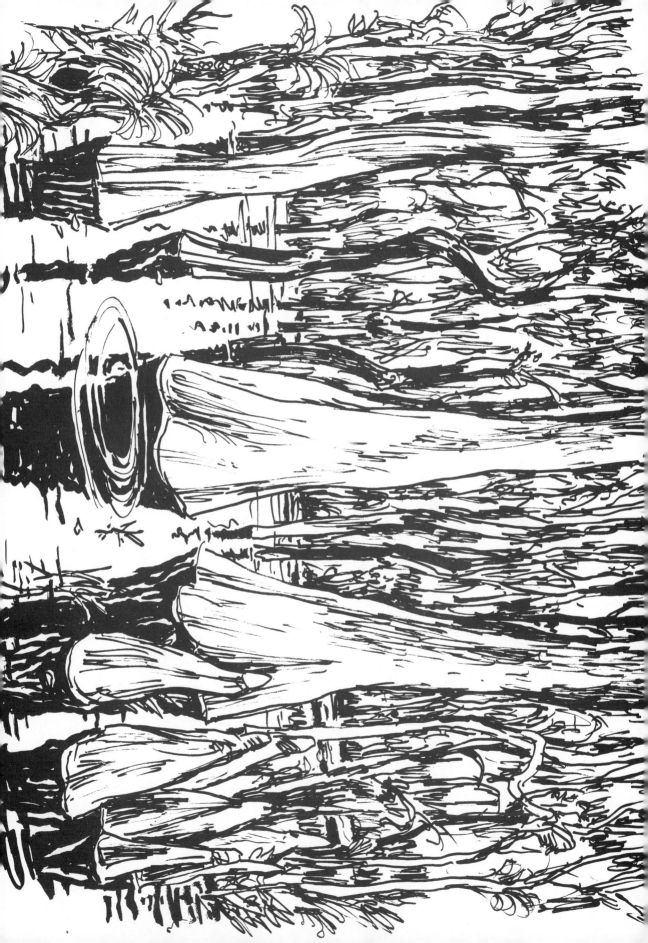

of all the plants and animals and building more on the land or not disposing properly of things harmful to it. But by doing so, I would lose and take from others riches God has given us for free that are far more valuable than money.

"We humans make ourselves poorer everytime we treat creatures like you as enemies to battle with and conquer. Anything God creates is on earth to bring unity and harmony and to improve all life. Without such creatures we cannot have the lives God wants us to have. So whenever we harm them, we harm ourselves at the same time. We reject what they are bringing us from God and make the earth less beautiful and healthy, less the place He is creating it to be.

"God is creating for us a wonderful home on which we can grow and create. He wants us to discover, enjoy, and share all He has brought about. Doing anything to make the earth less beautiful or healthy shows how ungrateful we are and how little we understand how important a beautiful and healthy earth is to having the best possible lives here.

"I believe that developing your wetland, Warren, did harm by interfering with the order and balance God is creating on earth. There were too many reasons it should have been protected. Not only did it cause rain to fall, but it collected water when the rains came and prevented the land around it from flooding. And as the water slowly sank underground, the wetland filtered it to remove dirt and make it good for creatures to drink. Having a place on earth which creates rain, prevents floods, and cleans water is much more important than developing your wetland. And that wetland gave food and shelter to creatures like you who cannot live anywhere else or who migrate through from other places on earth. Protecting you creatures who beautify the earth and give to others is also more important than developing your wetland. And your wetland was especially precious because humans already have destroyed so many of them. There may not be enough left to give to the earth all the things God created wetlands to give."

When the developer finished speaking, he joined the three as they traveled toward the surrounding countryside.

18.

Two new creatures appeared. One, a slow-moving gray animal with flippers, whiskers, and a flat tail shaped like a paddle, spoke first.

"Humans call me a manatee. For millions of years my gentle family has lived quietly in coastal waters and rivers eating plants. But then humans appeared and killed us with pollution, weapons, nets, and boats. And human development and pollution took away or poisoned most of our living space and food. Now there are few of us left and we may not live on earth much longer."

The second creature spoke next. She had long and heavy fur, a black and white body, and a white face with black nose, eye patches, and ears.

"Humans call me a panda. My family lives solitary lives eating bamboo in the high mountains of a small area of earth. But now humans are hunting us for our fur and taking away the land on which we live. There are few of us left and we may not live on earth much longer."

Yet the manatee and the panda told the others there were humans who loved them, and they led the group to a farm. The couple there was very happy to see them and explain how they live on the earth.

The woman spoke first.

"We love God, and we know He loves the earth. He is involved with everything here too much for us to claim we own any part of it. But taking care of the land on which we live and farm is a way we can show God we love Him and appreciate all the land gives us.

"When we first began to farm, we listened to humans who told us that to raise crops successfully, we needed to grow the same plants every year and use large amounts of water, poisons, chemicals, and special fertilizers. We did as they suggested and caused great harm. The poisons, chemicals, and fertilizers damaged our health and the health of our farmworkers, family, and neighbors. They prevented many crops which had grown here before from growing again. They hurt plants and animals above and below the soil who did not harm our crops or even helped them grow. They not only killed insects who damaged our crops but changed some into creatures who could do more damage. They harmed the water and creatures in it and the land into which they drained. Also we used so much water on our crops other creatures did not have the water they needed. And we planted so continually we were wearing out and losing the soil.

"We also listened to humans who told us that to produce eggs and meat, we needed to keep animals indoors in areas where we crowded together as many as we could. They even told us ways to make them grow faster than normal, like giving them drugs or controlling the length of their days with artificial lights in buildings without windows. We did all this and caused these animals great stress, boredom, discomfort, physical problems, and diseases. Sometimes they reacted to their suffering by

hurting themselves or others, making us do things like cutting off their beaks or tails. Then when they were either old enough or past the age of laying eggs or having babies, we shipped them away to be killed in ways that brought them more stress and pain.

"We indeed were producing many crops, eggs, and meat and making a great deal of money, but causing all this harm clearly showed us that we were not caring for the land and others. We felt guilty and separated from God. And even though we know Him well enough to realize that nothing we ever do will keep Him from loving us, we asked Him to forgive us and to teach us a better way to farm.

"We needed only to observe the world around us God is creating to discover the way to farm we wanted to follow. We learned that using harmful poisons, chemicals, and fertilizers was unnecessary and that we could raise a variety of crops and animals to fertilize the land and limit disease and insect damage. We learned also to control damaging insects with other insects, toads, lizards, birds, and our own hands, and to repel or attract them away by planting certain plants nearby. We learned to plant the crops which grow best in our area, fertilize the soil, and use less water. We also learned that our crops need much less water than we had used. And we learned that the land needs rest to help replenish the soil, and that we need to leave some land wild to have again in our lives the nonhuman creatures who previously lived here and traveled through.

"We saw too that God does not imprison or isolate creatures or cause them pain, disease, and discomfort. We found that other animals wanted to be healthy, comfortable, free, with others, and to care for their young in their own ways, just as we humans do. And we discovered ways to raise them in which we could relate to them and consider their needs. We now give them space outdoors in the sun and fresh air to roam and exercise and be with each other or have privacy. We feed them more natural and healthier food. We let mothers and their babies have the time they need to be together. We no longer give them drugs to make them grow faster or produce more milk. And we make sure any who must be killed die quickly and without pain."

Then the man spoke.

"Changing the way we farm and ending the harm we were causing made us so much happier. Not only are we making a good living, but our land and lives are worth more to us now than they ever have been. What we

56

produce is more healthful and better tasting. Wild animals have returned to the land and there is life again in the soil. We are no longer causing creatures God loves to suffer or doing harm to the water or soil. All this gives us great joy for it shows us we are caring for the earth more as God intends. And because we are living nearer to the way He does, we feel closer to Him than we ever have.

"Just as everything on earth feels God however it is able, we humans also feel His presence. But many ignore these feelings and believe humans can discover through science and technology all they need to understand about life. So these humans fail to get to know God and to learn about that part of life only He can teach them. Therefore they fail to learn all they can about themselves, others like you, or realize the earth is put together in love and must be treated lovingly. We humans will always need God. No matter how much we learn, we will never be as wise, powerful, or loving as He. While each one of us is different and can give to the earth what is special about us, if we are to improve life here, we need God's help. With that help, each can leave the earth a better place than it was before he or she lived on it.

"I feel you creatures and the earth are speaking to us. You are telling us that by treating you unlovingly, we are not only destroying you, but we are replacing who you are and what you bring with things which will destroy us - - poisoned air and water, unlimited industry and technology, sickness, poisoned and barren land, unrestricted population growth and development, loss of variety, and unsound ideas about growth, progress, and change. And because we are ignoring what you tell us about meaning, values, and understanding, we are replacing truth with ignorance."

When the farmers finished speaking, they accompanied the group as they journeyed toward a small community.

19.

Two more creatures appeared. The first to speak had thick, red fur and long arms with hands resembling those of the humans. Sensitive eyes highlighted her sad-looking hairless face.

"Humans call me an orangutan. My timid and peaceful family wandered through large forests for many generations eating vegetation and sleeping in the trees. But humans hunted us as enemies and captured us for zoos and circuses and to make into pets. And they cut down the forests in which we lived for homes, farms, and timber and finally forced us into

small island jungles. Now the humans are taking even those jungles. Soon there may be none of us on earth."

The orangutan's companion spoke next. He had four sturdy legs, a thin tail, and a heavy body covered with tough, dark skin. On his long face between his eyes and nose two large horns stood out prominently.

"Humans call me a rhinoceros. For ages my family has roamed large areas of the earth eating vegetation. But then humans wanted those areas for farms and to get them they killed almost all of us. And even the few of us who remain are being killed by humans who make our horns into cups and dagger handles or into powder some of them believe can make them more healthy and powerful than they really are. We will probably not live on earth much longer."

Yet the orangutan and the rhinoceros told the creatures there were humans who loved them, and they led the group to a house. The family there welcomed them warmly and were eager to share how they lived on the earth.

The father was the first to speak.

"I make a living harvesting seaweed. I am very careful to do nothing which would harm the water because it is so important to me and to the present and future of every creature on earth, including my own children. I do not speed on the water or dump garbage or oil into it, and I obey laws concerning the plants I harvest. And I make sure I do not use equipment which tears up the sea grasses, coral, or ocean bottom or harms creatures who live in and around the sea. I have never considered these creatures competitors. How empty the water and sky would be without them and how lonely and isolated we others would be without their companionship! Whenever I see humans harming the water or the creatures in or around it, I try to convince them to change their behavior or report them for violating any laws prohibiting such harm.

"If I harvested all the seaweed I could and did not care for others, I would make more money and have more possessions. Not long ago, others had convinced me and my family that humans improve ourselves only through having more than we need. But then we began to know God better and think for ourselves. We discovered that whenever we take more than we need, we are taking from others whom God loves and wants to share in what He has created. We began to understand that through the way we live and act toward the earth, either we will be helping treat all creatures with fairness or we will be helping treat them unjustly. We know now we humans progress only through becoming more as God wants us to be -- by valuing all others as He does, giving to, and sharing with them."

The mother then spoke.

"When I understood that God gives each human the opportunity to work with Him to make life on earth better, I began supporting causes for the protection of the order and balance He is creating here. I wrote letters to newspapers and got involved in community projects and decisions. Then because I came to feel that humans could better protect the earth and its creatures and that the laws already existing for their protection needed better enforcement, I became a politician. I quickly learned that most problems facing politicians do not have easy answers. But I have discovered they are solved with the greatest benefit when we work together toward finding solutions consistent with caring for the land and all creatures now and in the future. I know if politicians make decisions this way we are acting as God wants us to act, and I always ask Him for help in making these decisions."

The children spoke last.

"Our parents are teaching us to respect all creatures God creates and to understand that we are all related in one community. On many of our vacations we camp in areas uninhabited by humans. There we learn about plants and other animals and the worth of creatures like snakes, roaches, and vultures many humans do not value. From watching and studying nonhuman creatures we have learned that we humans have many things in common with them. And even though we may do some things better, like talk, think, and use tools, we have discovered their abilities often surpass ours or are unique. Some have better sight, hearing, or sense of smell. Some are stronger or faster. Some stand extreme temperatures or live longer. Some can fly or exist underwater. Some change colors or grow new limbs. Some are poisonous or use echoes to travel. We love learning these things and discussing them with our parents. We also help in our garden and care for the bushes and flowers we planted in our yard to attract insects and birds. We go to nature talks and parks and help with school and community environmental projects. Once we helped baby turtles hatching on developed beaches safely reach the sea. Another time we picked up litter

and planted native trees and wildflowers in the parks. And whenever we find an injured animal, we help it however we can. Someday we hope to help humans who feel they must do harm to others to survive find better ways to live."

The family told the group that they had discovered many ways to care for the earth and others. They had begun by considering how much they were taking from them. They quickly realized that they used and bought much more than they needed and that their desire to have was one reason business developed, farmed, ranched, mined, drilled, logged, and harvested so much of the earth. Possessions had complicated their lives and controlled most of what they thought about and did. They decided to free themselves from this. They gave many of their possessions away to those who did not have even what they needed and found many ways to conserve rather than consume. Now they did not waste electricity or water. They walked and bicycled many places and used car pools and public transportation. They bought as few sprays, poisons, plastics, and styrofoam as possible. They saved materials like steel cans, paper, aluminum, plastic, and glass for recycling. Whenever they could they bought recycled and nondisposable products and those with little packaging. They were careful

not to litter or dispose improperly of damaging waste like paints and motor oil. They bought their food locally. They purchased other necessities from and invested any savings with businesses showing concern for the earth and all creatures. And they supported groups organized to buy land uninhabited by humans, do research, lobby, and educate others about the earth.

All of them agreed that it had not been easy to stop considering first their own comfort, convenience, and security and begin thinking about the needs of others and how God wanted them to live. But when they had done so, they found their lives became more meaningful and content. They gained time to wonder, discover, create, and relate with others and with God. They felt so much closer to Him since they had made giving more important than taking. Because they wanted everyone to have the happiness and meaning they had found, they shared what they had learned with friends and neighbors and at their place of worship, schools, and clubs. Many listened and were glad to hear there were ways they could care for the earth and others. Some even made suggestions of their own -- eating grains and vegetables instead of meat; making compost from garbage; foregoing bigger and newer possessions; taking simpler vacations; using solar heating; doing without air conditioning; limiting family size; and

boycotting furs, leather, and products tested on animals. But many who heard had done nothing. Most were too afraid of making choices and changes. They refused to see that they were making choices -- not to do , not to know, not to care, not to find out how they could make a difference.

The family joined the group as they traveled toward a beautiful meadow filled with wildflowers and birdsong and surrounded by mountains.

20.

Two new creatures appeared. One, a muscular human with dark hair and eyes who wore only a loincloth, spoke first.

"Other humans call me an Indian. My ancestors were the first humans to live in a great forest of trees, vegetation, and vines where powerful rivers flow and countless plants and animals live. My tribe lives there still in small groups traveling around hunting for food and building shelters in which to sleep, eat, and visit. We speak our own language and have our own customs, skills, and arts. Over the years we have lived in the forest, we have learned much about how the lives of its plants and animals are connected to each other and to us. We respect the creatures with whom we share the forest and believe we do not own it but are cared for by it. And, most important to us, it is where we meet God. But now we are being harassed and killed by other humans who feel differently about the land and its creatures. They are capturing and killing the creatures and destroying the forest with chainsaws, fires, diseases, floods, and poisons. The forest, my tribe, and most of the other forest creatures may not live on earth much longer."

The Indian held in his hand the last creature to speak -- a plant with yellow-green leaves forming the shape of a fan. At its top were several large blue blossoms of striking beauty.

"Humans call me an orchid. My family has grown for ages clinging to the branches of small trees in the foothills of a great mountain range. But then we were discovered by humans who collected us or sold us for large profits. They stripped us from the trees and shipped us all around the world. Many of us died from lack of care or proper surroundings both during these journeys and after reaching foreign lands. Now where once we were abundant, very few exist. Soon all of us on the earth will live only as captives."

Yet the Indian and the orchid told the creatures there were humans who loved them, and they led the group to a place of worship on the edge of a deep, blue lake.

The religious leaders there joyfully welcomed them and shared their knowledge of the relationship between God and the creatures on earth.

"There are some humans who say they do not believe God exists. If they would only learn even a little about the order and balance of the life He is creating here, they would understand that these things are not accidents and that their Creator is far more wise and powerful than any creature on earth. Perhaps discovering that will make them curious about Him. And by finding out more about Him, they will learn that He is also far more loving than any creature on earth, and that His wisdom and power come from that love. But the most wonderful thing they will discover is that He loves us and wants to help us to become as loving and wise and powerful as we can. He even wants to help each of us contribute the specialness we possess to the order and balance He is creating here!

"There are many humans who believe that even if God exists, He is somewhere else. To them the earth is either a place from which they want

to escape to be with Him or a place to make over to bring Him here. But we see God here every moment. We believe He is everywhere -- that all God creates is part of Him and that part of Him is in all He creates. We see Him not only in the acts of the humans He is teaching to love, but in the smell of the Spring meadow, the howl of the wolf, the touch of the snowflake, the taste of the wild raspberry, and the sight of the tiny oak sprouting from the acorn. He has shown us how deeply He loves us. And He has shown us He will never leave us alone or fail to take us back those countless times we push Him away. He is here where we are, reaching out to those who do not know Him and helping those who do find joy, peace, understanding, forgiveness, and hope.

"Any creature -- a rock, a snake, an insect, a river -- who reflects God inside it nurtures all who see it. We can see God in a wood stork flying over the wetland and in the wetland over which the wood stork flies. Both remind us that God is creating a place unique in all the universe filled with creatures who bring beauty, health, variety, fun, surprise, and mystery and who keep us from being dull, insensitive, and full of pride. Nonhuman creatures give us insights and feelings we cannot find in our human world.

And they tell us so much about God. On the one hand, they help us see how great He is and how limited our abilities are. Yet on the other, they empower us to help Him create through using the abilities we do have. From nonhuman creatures we have learned much about how to live on earth and how we can improve life for others. But we humans have lived on earth such a short time. We have yet to discover most of what it and its creatures bring and most of the ways they can help us make the earth a better place.

"Sometimes we forget that the earth is not ours and that we are not the only creatures of worth on it. We feel that because we humans can relate to God in a unique way that we are separate from nonhumans and that they are of little worth. We could not be more wrong! We have understood for thousands of years that God loves all creatures. That alone gives them worth. But they are worthy also because they are able to relate to God and enrich the lives of others in ways humans cannot. Their worthiness like ours comes from connection to God and to all others.

"When we destroy the natural world and create things which separate us from it, we so easily forget our connections to the land and other

75

creatures. We forget that the same One has created us. We forget that He has made us only one member of a community which includes everything He has created -- the other animals, plants, soil, air, water. We forget that we are so united with them that without them we would not survive. We fail to remember that they are like our brothers and sisters and that the earth out of whose material we are made and who provides for us is like our mother. We fail to let them help us find meaning and values and to listen to what they have to tell us about how they need to be treated -- how they need to be loved. And we fail to understand that the way we treat them affects us all.

"When we love God and let Him teach us how to love we discover we can love all creatures and that all creatures can be loved. And we find that, unless we love all creatures, we cannot completely love even other humans or God. We learn that loving means not crowding you creatures off the earth or sacrificing you for things like fashion, entertainment, or money. Instead loving means helping you and all of God's creatures to be whomever you can and to enjoy your lives and improve life for others however you are able. And whenever we humans act toward you with love in this way, others can see

God in us!

"We disagree with many humans who believe that caring for the earth and its creatures is a job God has given to humans. We care for the earth and its creatures as God wants us to only when we understand how good He is, how much He loves us, and that all He is creating comes from His love. When we understand these things, we care for God and others not because we have to care, but because we want to care -- not out of any duty to God, but out of love for Him and all He is creating. Caring out of love is the way God cares. There can be no better way for us to live on the earth!"

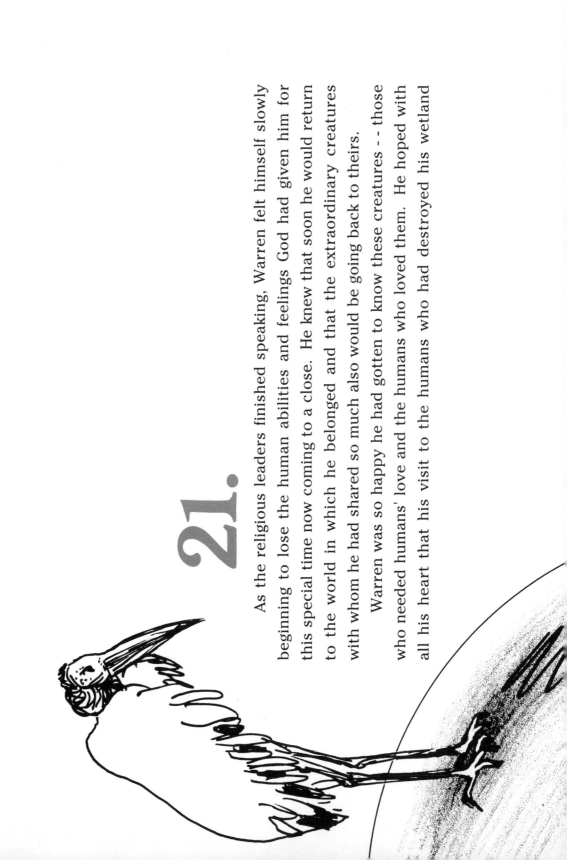

21.

As the religious leaders finished speaking, Warren felt himself slowly beginning to lose the human abilities and feelings God had given him for this special time now coming to a close. He knew that soon he would return to the world in which he belonged and that the extraordinary creatures with whom he had shared so much also would be going back to theirs.

Warren was so happy he had gotten to know these creatures -- those who needed humans' love and the humans who loved them. He hoped with all his heart that his visit to the humans who had destroyed his wetland would help them begin to understand that only through knowing God and giving love to all others will they find real happiness and meaning.

While the creatures left one by one, the developer, the farmers, the family members, and the religious leaders put their arms around each other. Watching them go was the most difficult thing they had ever done. It meant the end of these unique moments of God's nearness and love and the connection between His creatures. And it made them realize how much they longed to ensure these wonderful beings a future of celebration instead of suffering.

Warren waited until last to leave. He looked intently into the eyes of each human one final time before leaping quickly into the sky. For as long as he was able, he soared majestically overhead, lifting up their hearts as they watched from the meadow, and telling them goodbye in the best way he knew.

No one but God saw his tears.

The End

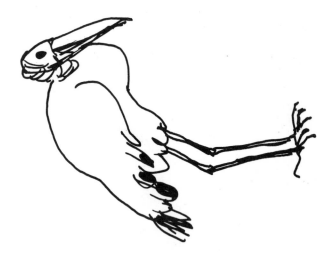